# Landslides

by Jeffrey Zuehlke

PULL AHEAD BOOKS
Forces of Nature

Lerner Publications Company • Minneapolis

**Photo Acknowledgments**

The images in this book are used with the permission of: © Reuters/CORBIS, p. 4; © Urs Flueeler/epa/CORBIS, p. 6; AP Photo/Chandra Karki, p. 7; © Handout/Malacanang/Reuters/CORBIS, p. 8; AP Photo/John Moore, p. 10; © David McNew/Getty Images, p. 11; © Bill Banaszewski/Visuals Unlimited, p. 12; © Daniel and Flossie White/Alamy, p. 13; © Marli Miller/Visuals Unlimited, p. 14; AP Photo/Dado Galdieri, p. 15; © Picture Contact/Alamy, p. 16; AP Photo/Fabrice Coffrini, p. 18; AP Photo/Zhou Wenjie, Xinhua, p. 19; © Steve Vidler/Super Stock, p. 20; © Des Westmore/Alamy, p. 22; © age fotostock/SuperStock, p. 23; AP Photo/Murad Sezer, p. 24; AP Photo/ Trisnadi, p. 25; © Stringer/AFP/Getty Images, p. 26; © Rico Gonzales/AFP/Getty Images, p. 27; U.S. Geological Survey/photo by Tom Casadevall, p. 28.
Front Cover: AP Photo/La Prensa Grafica

Lerner Publications Company
A division of Lerner Publishing Group, Inc.
241 First Avenue North
Minneapolis, MN 55401 U.S.A.

Website address: www.lernerbooks.com

Words in **bold type** are explained in a glossary on page 31.

Library of Congress Cataloging-in-Publication Data

Zuehlke, Jeffrey, 1968–
    Landslides / by Jeffrey Zuehlke.
        p.    cm. – (Pull ahead books—forces of nature)
    Includes index.
    ISBN 978-0-8225-8831-3 (lib. bdg. : alk. paper)
    1. Landslides—Juvenile literature. I. Title.
QE599.A2Z85 2009
551.3'07–dc22                              2007046066
                        0510

Manufactured in the United States of America
1 2 3 4 5 6 – BP – 14 13 12 11 10 09

# Table of Contents

# What Is a Landslide?

Where did all this rock and dirt come from? A **landslide** has struck this area. Rock, dirt, and **debris** slid down the mountain. The landslide buried homes and trees.

Some landslides move slowly. People have time to get out of the way.

Other landslides move very fast. The whole side of this mountain rolled down. Dirt and rocks smashed everything in their path.

Too much rain caused this landslide in the Philippines in 2003.

# Where and When Landslides Happen

Landslides can strike wherever there are mountains or hills.  They often happen when there has been too much rain.  The land becomes very wet and heavy.  It starts to slide downhill.

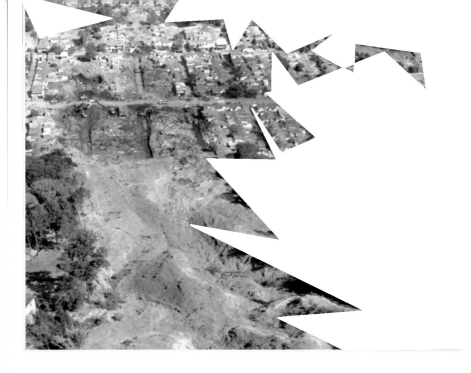

Sometimes **earthquakes** cause landslides. An earthquake is a shaking movement of the ground. Land shakes loose. It slides downhill.

People can cause landslides too. Sometimes people clear trees and plants from hillsides.

Trees and plants have **roots** that grow below the ground. The roots hold the dirt and rocks together.

But what if people clear too many trees
and plants?  The land has nothing to
hold it together.  The dirt and rocks
become loose.

Wind or rain can wash the rocks downhill. It happens a little at a time. This is called **erosion**.

But sometimes, the loose rock and dirt come down all at once. Then it is a landslide.

# A Landslide Strikes

Sometimes a landslide strikes with no warning.  Suddenly, the side of a mountain comes roaring down.  The debris rushes down very quickly.  The landslide is heavy and fast.  Nothing can stop it.

Rescue teams use a dog to search for people after a landslide.

Landslides can bury people and animals. **Rescue teams** rush in to help. The teams use dogs to help them.

**Survivors** might be buried under debris. The dogs can smell survivors. The dogs show the rescuers where to dig.

People who live on hills or mountains can watch for signs of a landslide.

# Staying Safe

How can you know if a landslide is coming? Landslides often strike fast. But people can watch for warning signs. These are clues that the land is starting to slide.

People can keep an eye on trees
and signposts. Have they suddenly
tipped or moved? This might be a
clue that the land is slipping.

Cracks can also be a warning sign. You may see new cracks in walls, roads, or land. Tell an adult about these warning signs.

You may see or hear a landslide coming. If you do, leave the area.

These children practice leaving their school.

If you can't escape, stay calm. Go to
the top floor of your home or building.
Crouch under a table or sturdy furniture.

Rescue workers search near a landslide.

Stay where you are until the landslide is over. Then leave if it is safe to do so. Or wait for a rescue team to come help you.

Scientists study landslides. They watch for warning signs. Their job is to keep people safe.

# MORE ABOUT LANDSLIDES

The largest landslide ever recorded happened in Washington State. In 1980, Mount Saint Helens volcano erupted. It caused a giant mudflow. The powerful eruption also blew off the top of the mountain. That created a landslide that tumbled more than 13 miles (21km)!

# Tools to Detect Landslides

• **Geologists** have made tools that check for signs of landslides.  One tool is the acoustic flow monitor.  An acoustic flow monitor can sense changes in the sound the land is making.  The changes warn scientists that the land is moving.

• The tiltmeter is another special tool.  It measures changes in the tilt, or steepness, of mountains and hills.  Scientists drill tiltmeters into hills.  The tiltmeter sends signals.  The signals show if a mountain or hill is moving.

• Geologists also use satellites to watch for warning signs.  Satellites spin far above Earth.  They take pictures of the land.  Geologists study the pictures carefully.  The pictures can give them clues that the land is changing.

# Further Reading

## Books

Goodwin, Peter. *Landslides, Slumps, and Creeps*. New York: Franklin Watts, 1997.

Nelson, Robin. *Gravity*. Minneapolis: Lerner Publications Company, 2004.

Redmond, Jim, and Roberta Redmond. *Landslides and Avalanches*. New York: Raintree, 2002.

## Websites

### Ask an Earth-Scientist
http://www.soest.hawaii.edu/GG/ASK/askanerd.html
Send a question about landslides to a geologist at the University of Hawaii.

### Geology of Mars:  Landslides
http://www.lukew.com/marsgeo/landslides.html
Landslides don't just happen on Earth.  Visit this site to see pictures of a landslide on the planet Mars.

### Mount Saint Helens
http://www.kidscosmos.org/kid-stuff/kids-volcanoes-st-helens.html
Learn about the eruption of Mount Saint Helens, which caused a giant landslide.

# Glossary

**debris:** loose soil, rock, or other objects

**detect:** to sense or find out

**earthquakes:** a shaking of the ground caused by moving rock

**erosion:** the slow wearing away of rock and soil

**geologists:** scientists who study Earth

**landslide:** a mass of soil and rock that breaks loose from a mountain, hill, or cliff and slides down

**rescue teams:** teams that are trained to help people after a disaster

**roots:** the parts of plants and trees that grow under the ground

**survivors:** people who have lived through a disaster

# Index

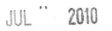